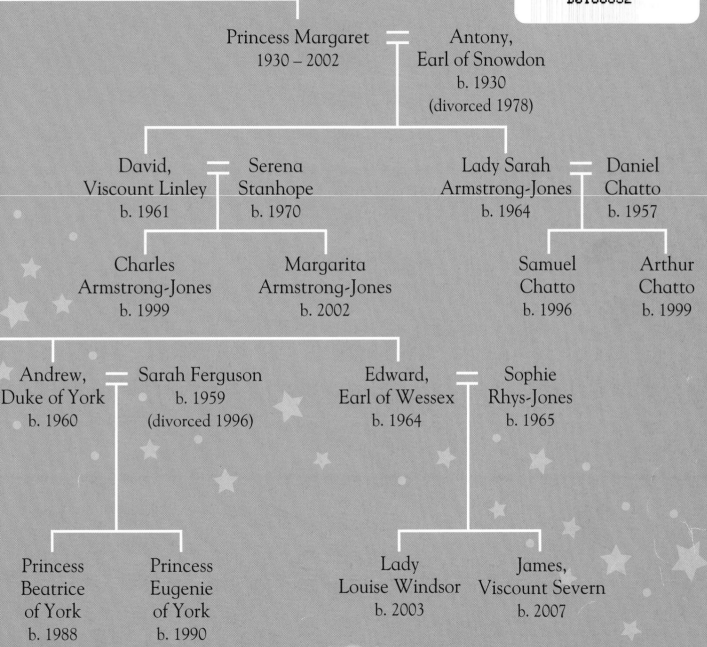

Princess Margaret
1930 – 2002

Antony,
Earl of Snowdon
b. 1930
(divorced 1978)

David,
Viscount Linley
b. 1961

Serena
Stanhope
b. 1970

Lady Sarah
Armstrong-Jones
b. 1964

Daniel
Chatto
b. 1957

Charles
Armstrong-Jones
b. 1999

Margarita
Armstrong-Jones
b. 2002

Samuel
Chatto
b. 1996

Arthur
Chatto
b. 1999

Andrew,
Duke of York
b. 1960

Sarah Ferguson
b. 1959
(divorced 1996)

Edward,
Earl of Wessex
b. 1964

Sophie
Rhys-Jones
b. 1965

Princess
Beatrice
of York
b. 1988

Princess
Eugenie
of York
b. 1990

Lady
Louise Windsor
b. 2003

James,
Viscount Severn
b. 2007

WILLIAM

The bridegroom prince in our real-life fairy tale was born in London on 21 June 1982. He is the older of two sons born to Charles, the Prince of Wales and the late Diana, Princess of Wales. Prince William Arthur Philip Louis is second in line to the throne.

When William was 13, he followed in the footsteps of many other members of royal families across the world by attending Eton College. It was whilst William was at school, and only 15 years old, that tragedy struck when his mother was killed in a terrible car accident in Paris.

William and his younger brother, Harry, attempted to come to terms with the loss of their mother as they continued their education. William went on to St Andrews University in Scotland, and it was here that he first caught sight of the girl who would become such a huge part of his young life.

KATE

Catherine Elizabeth Middleton was born not that far away from William, in Berkshire, on 9 January 1982. She has two younger siblings, Philippa and James. Her parents are Michael and Carole Middleton and the family still live in the home where the three Middleton children were brought up.

Kate was educated at Marlborough College, after which she made her way up to Scotland to read History of Art at St Andrews University. Little could she have realized the significance of choosing St Andrews, and how this decision would change the course of her life.

Amongst her friends, Kate has long had the reputation of being a kind, sensible and quietly competent young woman. These are qualities that she will find invaluable as she prepares to take the first exciting, yet daunting steps towards becoming the wife of a future king.

UNIVERSITY YEARS

University is an exciting time, with new friends to meet and a new place to live. It was just the same for William and Kate, who met, through an old school friend of Kate's, at the beginning of their first year. They found themselves on the same course, reading History of Art, and having a few friends in common, soon became firm friends. It helped that they were also in the same Hall of Residence, St Salvator's or 'Sallies' as it is known.

As their first year ended, William and Kate decided to find a house in the town, choose some flatmates to split the rent with, and share.

Although William and Kate would be nothing more than friends for some time to come, the future king's head was certainly turned when Kate took part in a charity fashion show at St Andrews. He suddenly developed an unlikely interest in high fashion, and reputedly paid £200 for a front row seat. He was in the perfect position to watch Kate sashay down the catwalk in a stunning black lace dress.

The university that dominates the quiet seaside town of St Andrews in Fife enjoys something of a reputation as a good place to meet a future husband or wife, with one in ten students reportedly meeting that special someone during their time there! Perhaps it was the romance of the wind-swept beaches or something in the ancient stones – this famous university was founded in 1413 – that sowed the seed of romance between William and Kate.

ROMANCE BLOSSOMS

As he began his second year of studies, William was beginning to wonder if his life was heading in the right direction. He became disillusioned with university life, and wasn't particularly enjoying his course. Being the heir to the throne, even in a sleepy town in Scotland, made William an obvious target for journalists. Although there was a 'gentleman's agreement' with the press to leave William alone to study, word seemed to get out whenever he was seen with a girlfriend, even a non-romantic one. Being a sensitive, modern and down-to-earth prince, William hated the idea that any female friend of his (and their unsuspecting family) could wake up one morning to find their lawn being trampled by hundreds of waiting paparazzi.

It was William's friend and flatmate, Kate, who helped him through this difficult time. She was instrumental in persuading the reluctant student to change to a different course, Geography, and stay to complete his studies. And so it was that William, Kate and their two flatmates took turns shopping for groceries, hosted wild dinner parties and generally enjoyed student life for the next couple of years.

During their third year at university, William and Kate enjoyed a skiing holiday in the very romantic Swiss resort of Klosters, the long-favoured ski destination of Prince Charles and his family (Prince Charles even has a cable car there named after him!). They were surrounded by friends and family and yet the long lenses of the press still managed to capture a glance here and a joke there. The fairy tale-loving public back in rainy Britain were easily convinced that a royal romance was slowly developing in the snow and the Alpine air!

With the romantic dreams of the world being directed towards William and Kate, it was easy to forget how young they still were. William was beginning to get fed up with the attention, and took the opportunity to point out firmly during a press call that he was very much a single man, and only twenty-two. At the same time he silenced the rumours by stating that he would not think about getting married until he was twenty-eight or even thirty.

GROWING CLOSER

William's father, The Prince of Wales, was married to Camilla Parker Bowles on 9 April 2005. Although the eyes of the world were on the royal family at this long-expected royal celebration, Kate was notable by her absence. Perhaps William didn't want to detract attention from Charles and his new bride, or perhaps it was too big a step to take, on too big a stage, for this point in their fledgling relationship.

A few weeks after his father's wedding came the wedding of one of William's oldest friends, Hugh van Cutsem. This time Kate was there too, and although they arrived and left separately, they were very much together during the day. It was a high-society occasion, full of old family friends of William, and Kate's inclusion was a sure sign that she was becoming more and more important in his life.

Later in the summer of 2005, William and Kate donned caps and gowns at their graduation ceremony, in front of William's proud grandmother, the Queen. As a sign of their growing friendship, the couple's parents hosted a joint lunch party afterwards to celebrate.

William and Kate's relationship was growing in strength, and a public kiss on the slopes of Klosters the following January showed the world that the pair were more than just good friends.

REALITY HITS

However, it was time for life to become more serious. Just days after their romantic get away in Klosters, William entered the Royal Military Academy, Sandhurst, where generations of royalty from every corner of the world have been turned into ultra-fit and ultra-tough army officers during the gruelling, year-long training.

While Kate waited for her handsome soldier to complete his training, she set about finding a career for herself. With her History of Art degree, she was keen to find work in a London gallery, but was disappointed to discover that her royal connections brought only unwelcome paparazzi to their doors. Changing tack slightly, she secured a job as an accessories buyer for an upmarket high street fashion chain. But her life was made difficult by the hounding she received from the press. Lawyers were consulted and complaints made about the constant harassment. Even when William whisked Kate off on holiday to the hideaway island of Mustique in the Caribbean, the long lenses of the press managed to seek them out.

A ROLLERCOASTER OF EMOTION

The combination of William's exhausting army training and the intrusion of the press into Kate's life led to the sad news, in April 2007, of the end of their relationship. Perhaps it was inevitable that the intense atmosphere they were both living in would prove too difficult to handle. The two of them were privately devastated, but this time apart was to prove a useful break, as it gave them both the opportunity for reflection as well as some welcome breathing space.

Within a few months, it became apparent that William and Kate could not stay apart and they were soon a couple once more. They had shared such a lot together and had realized that they cared too much to throw it all away.

In May 2008, William's cousin, Peter Phillips, married Autumn Kelly at Windsor Castle. Although Prince William could not attend, Kate was present, and it was here that the Queen, keen to meet the young woman who had stolen her grandson's heart, sought her out to exchange a few private words.

New Roles

The young couple were very much together at this time. Whilst many of their friends were tying the knot, they were keen to strike out and achieve goals for themselves before settling down to family life. William decided not to pursue a career in the army, but instead to undergo training as a pilot. In April 2008, Kate accompanied Prince William when he was awarded his RAF wings at the Royal Air Force College, Cranwell.

Kate, meanwhile, was working hard on increasing the success of the Middleton family business. Along with her sister, brother, and their parents, she helped run their popular party planning company.

The Proposal

In October 2010, William and Kate set off on holiday to one of the prince's favourite places. William has always felt at home in Africa. It is where he is free from the cameras and questions about his future. On 20 October, in an isolated and spartan log cabin with no electricity, few people and no distractions, William felt it was the time to ask the most important question of his life.

The hideaway cabins at Rutundu, north of Nairobi, are very remote. They can be reached only by air or horseback and the nearest road is fifteen kilometres away. William and Kate's security was provided by the wandering elephants, leopards, hyenas and buffalo! Having first visited the same spot a couple of years before, had William been pondering this moment since then?

William's mother, Diana, is always close to her eldest son's heart, and she certainly was on this special day as William took the sapphire and diamond ring his father had given her thirty years before and slipped it onto Kate's finger. The future king was so organized, and had been preparing for this moment for so long, that he had been carrying the priceless ring around with him in his backpack for the previous three weeks!

It must have been so hard for the happy couple to keep their secret to themselves. They signed the guestbook at the cabins without giving a clue as to what had just happened and returned home with no one but extremely close family any the wiser. An official engagement would now have to be planned and announced to a waiting world.

THE SECRET'S OUT

On 16 November 2010, a simply worded press release from Clarence House – the official residence of the Prince of Wales and his family – announced the forthcoming marriage between William and Catherine, as she will be known.

The couple gave a light-hearted and relaxed interview on the same day. William and Kate were happy to chat and giggle about his lack of expertise in the kitchen, and his fear of asking Kate's father for her hand in marriage in case he said no!

"There's a true romantic in there!"

Kate on William

"I, at the time, wasn't very happy about it, but actually it made me a stronger person."

Kate on the temporary break-up of their relationship

"I would have loved to have met her. She's obviously an inspirational woman to look up to."

Kate on Diana, Princess of Wales

"No one is trying to fill my mother's shoes."

William on Kate

"It is just really easy being with each other."

William on Kate

"When I first met Kate I knew there was something very special about her."

William on Kate

ALWAYS IN THEIR HEARTS

Princess Diana was always very determined to bring up her boys in a modern way. She did not believe in hiring governesses who would keep William and Harry out of sight in the palace, and insisted that they attend a nursery school from the age of three. She was keen they should feel comfortable in the company of others, and experience the rough and tumble of the playground.

William was very close to his mother. She would have loved the royal wedding build-up, and felt proud that the woman her beloved son has chosen to spend his life with will stand by his side wearing her ring. William said of presenting Kate with his mother's ring: "Obviously she's not going to be around to share any of the fun and excitement of it all – this was my way of keeping her close to it all."

ROYAL REACTIONS

The royal family must have been
waiting for William and Kate's
engagement announcement just
as the public were, and many have
spoken openly about their joy.
William's brother, Harry, poignantly spoke
of now having a sister – something he had
always wanted. The news was greeted
with enormous pleasure by William's
grandmother the Queen, and his father
Charles – although Charles couldn't
prevent himself from saying that the news
made him feel very old!

WORLDWIDE CELEBRATIONS

News of the royal engagement had reached every corner of the globe within seconds of the official announcement. In the midst of a worldwide global recession the wedding is seen as a joyful event that will give everyone a lift in 2011. Newspapers across the world have carried images of the smiling couple and everyone is anticipating a fabulous party!

Around the world, people love the pomp and ceremony that Britain has always been known for. On the big day, the world will be looking forward to the parades, the horses, the carriages and the polished breastplates of the Guards.

But even more than this, people will be pleased that William is marrying the woman he so clearly loves. The couple's obvious happiness and love for each other is what everyone will be waiting to see.

KATE, QUEEN OF FASHION

So far, Kate has shown a classic and understated elegance. Although she does not enjoy being the centre of attention, she is careful how she dresses, aware that there are photographers ready to capture every choice she makes. Kate has a natural sense of what suits her and generally sticks to simple, well-cut designs in unfussy fabrics.

Although Kate loves to dress up in beautiful designer gowns, she is also a fan of high street fashion. She famously wore a dress from Topshop on her twenty-fifth birthday – which then sold out within hours!

WESTMINSTER ABBEY

The Royal Wedding will take place at Westminster Abbey in London on 29 April 2011. The day has been declared a public holiday so everyone can join in the celebrations. The abbey can accommodate just over 2,000 guests, which will include many heads of state from around the world.

Westminster Abbey was chosen as the venue because of its staggering beauty as well as its thousand-year royal history. There has been a tradition of worship on this site since the middle of the tenth century, even though the abbey as we know it was not established until 1245, built by Henry III. It has been used for coronations since 1066, when William the Conqueror was crowned on Christmas Day, and is also the final resting place for seventeen monarchs.

The abbey will also hold poignant memories for William. It was here in 1997 that his mother's funeral took place. He will remember that one million people in mourning lined the streets that day to wish her farewell, and he will be pleased to now have some truly happy memories of the abbey to hold alongside such sad ones.

A History of Royal Weddings

There have been fourteen royal weddings held at Westminster Abbey, the first being in the year 1100 between Henry I and Princess Matilda of Scotland in a church that preceded today's abbey.

The Queen Mother married HRH The Duke of York in 1923 at Westminster Abbey. The crowds, all those years ago, lined the same streets as their grandchildren and great grandchildren will, to cheer and wave at the royal wedding.

The wedding of the Queen and Prince Philip on 20 November 1947 was a real reason for celebration, coming so soon after the austerity of World War II. The bride and groom were well aware that rationing was still in place and were careful that the day, whilst full of celebrations and street parties, was not ostentatious.

Prince Charles and Lady Diana Spencer chose St Paul's cathedral for their wedding on 29 July 1981, it is thought simply because of its size – there were 3,500 guests! It is difficult to imagine how the bride, aged just nineteen, must have felt on that day in her ivory taffeta gown and long train with tens of millions of eyes focused upon her. The day was sealed perfectly when, on the balcony of Buckingham Palace, Charles turned to kiss his new bride.

William's uncle, Prince Andrew, married Sarah Ferguson on 23 July 1986 at the abbey. There were four bridesmaids and four page boys, one of whom was a mischievous four-year-old Prince William, who couldn't resist teasing the bridesmaid next to him!

William's youngest uncle, Prince Edward, married Sophie Rhys-Jones at St George's Chapel in Windsor on 19 June 1999. Although this was quite a low-key affair, with no ceremonial or military involvement, the wedding was still attended by 550 guests and watched by a worldwide television audience of 200 million!

Prince Charles remarried in 2005, eight years after the death of William's mother Diana. His bride was Camilla Parker Bowles, whom he had known for more than thirty years. Compared to Charles' first wedding, it was a quiet event. After a simple civil ceremony in Windsor,

a blessing took place at St George's Chapel in Windsor Castle followed by a reception for 800 guests. The couple drove off for their honeymoon in a car that William and Harry had covered with foam that spelled out 'Prince', 'Duchess' and 'Just Married'!

The Future

After the excitement of their wedding and honeymoon, William and Kate will return to their busy lives. William will continue with his career as a search and rescue pilot with the RAF, while Kate will settle back into life at their farmhouse in North Wales, near William's RAF base. They lead a simpler life there, away from the spotlight, which seems to suit them both.

Who knows when William and Kate will be King and Queen? When that day comes, they will have a challenging, busy and very much more public life to settle into, but until then they seem happy tucked away together in a quiet Welsh valley.

Both William and Kate have expressed publicly their wish to start a family of their own in due course. But they will not be pressured, as they are young and there is plenty of time. When William was asked about their plans for a family he drily replied, "I think we'll take it one step at a time. We'll get over the marriage first, and then maybe look at the kids."

Official portrait photograph for the engagement of Prince William and Miss Catherine Middleton.
© Copyright 2010 Mario Testino.

♥ ♥ ♥ ♥ ♥ ♥ ♥ ♥

CREDITS

A catalogue record for this book is available from the British Library
Published by Ladybird Books Ltd
A Penguin Company
Penguin Books Ltd., 80 Strand, London WC2R 0RL, UK
Penguin Books Australia Ltd., Camberwell, Victoria, Australia
Penguin Group (NZ) 67 Apollo Drive, Rosedale, North Shore 0632, New Zealand

001 – 10 9 8 7 6 5 4 3 2 1

PICTURE CREDITS